Ceres in Astrology

Nourishment, Power, and the Rebirth of the Feminine

"She came not to be found, but to be remembered."

Louise Edington

Sacred Threads
Imprint

Ceres in Astrology: Nourishment, Power, and the Rebirth of the Feminine

© 2025 Louise Edington
Published by Sacred Threads Imprint
www.sacredthreadsimprint.com

All rights reserved. No part of this publication may be reproduced, stored, or transmitted in any form without prior permission of the publisher, except for brief quotations used in reviews or scholarly work. Cover and interior design by Louise Edington with assistance from AI support.

Paperback ISBN: 978-1-968202-00-2
Ebook ISBN: 978-1-968202-01-9

First published: August 12, 2025

Book design by Sarah E. Holroyd (https://sleepingcatbooks.com)

Sacred Threads
Imprint

Praise for Ceres in Astrology

"With Ceres on her own Ascendant, Louise Edington has lived the story she tells here. There are fresh, clear, human insights on every page. Watch as she brings to a light a planet that has been hidden in plain sight for over two centuries."

~Steven Forrest, author of The Inner Sky

"This multifaceted, beautifully written guide to Ceres deserves a place in every Western astrological library. Louise Edington masterfully weaves Ceres' mythology, astrological history, and personal, generational and collective implications into a powerful argument for promoting her to inner planet status. Bonus for readers who track aspects to critical or sensitized degrees: Louise's research will blow you away, as it did me."

~Kathy Biehl, astrologer & author

"If we are to create, to thrive, to blossom, to LIVE, then we need to know our natal Ceres. Louise's homage to the Earth Mother gives us an opportunity to deeply explore and embody this powerful and essential archetype. Just as we evolve, so does our astrology. I believe this book will become a classic on the astrologer's bookshelf."

~Leah Whitehorse, Astrologer and Writer

Welcome to the Return of the Mother

Ceres in Astrology is not just a book. It's a remembering. A reclamation. A weaving back into the rhythms of care, grief, and renewal.

May it nourish your path, awaken your roots, and guide your work with the stars.

Ceres in Astrology: Nourishment, Power, and the Rebirth of the Feminine

Exploring the Astrological Significance of Ceres and the Divine Feminine

How to Use This Book

This book is designed to be both a sacred companion and a practical guide. You may choose to read it from beginning to end, following the arc of Ceres' myth, re-emergence, and astrological meanings—or you may open it intuitively to the sections that call you most.

- If you're new to astrology: begin with the signs and houses chapters (Parts 6–7) to understand how Ceres shows up in your own chart.
- If you're an experienced astrologer: dive into the discovery and reclassification charts, aspects, and generational themes for deeper archetypal context.
- Use the Blending Aspects section as a reference whenever Ceres makes contact with another planet in a natal or transiting chart.

This is a living text. You are invited to mark it, meditate with it, teach from it, and return to it in cycles—just like Ceres herself.

May it nourish you and the world you help reweave.

Contents

Foreword	xi
Introduction	1
Part 1: My Personal Journey with Ceres	**3**
My Ceres Awakening	5
The Hidden Mother	5
The Unraveling and the Realignment	6
Threads of My Story	6
The Offering	8
Part 2: Who Is Ceres? Understanding Her Place in Astrology	**9**
Discovery and Reclassification	11
Planetary Significance	11
NASA Discoveries	12
The Titius-Bode Law and Planetary Alignment	12
A New Planetary Pairing	12
Reclaiming Astrological Importance	13
The Sacred Waters	13
A New Model for Astrology	13
Thresholds and Time: The Evolution of Ceres	14
Part 3: Astrological Insights—Ceres as Catalyst for Consciousness	**17**
The Discovery Chart of Ceres: A Threshold Moment	19
The Reclassification Chart: A Continuation of the Myth	21
Ceres and the Outer Planets: Generational Signatures	23
Transition: From Generations to Guardianship	27
Reimagining Rulership: Ceres, Taurus, and Virgo	27
The Symbol of Ceres	28
Part 4: The Mythology of Ceres and Demeter	**29**
Ceres, Excess, and the Cry for Redemption	33
Part 5: Archetypal and Psychological Significance	**35**
The Archetypes of Ceres: The Mother's Many Faces	37
Mother Wound and Attachment Theory	38
Psychological Depth: Jungian Insights and Internal Family Systems (IFS)	39
Quantum, Energetic, and Archetypal Healing: Inner to Outer	

Integration	40
Part 6: Ceres in Our Collective Evolution	**41**
Ceres and the Industrial Revolution	43
Climate Crisis, Displacement, and Refugee Crises: Modern Manifestations of Ceres	43
Societal Disconnection Mirroring Personal Disconnection	44
A Vision for Healing Through Ceres Consciousness	44
Part 7: Working with Ceres in Your Natal Chart	**47**
Understanding Ceres by Sign, House, and Aspect	49
Ceres as Wound and Gift	50
Keywords for Ceres:	51
Practical Reflections and Chart Examples	52
Your Ceres Questions	52
Transition: From Generations to Guardianship	53
Reimagining Rulership: Ceres, Taurus, and Virgo	54
Ceres through the Signs, Houses, and Aspects	54
Ceres through the Signs	55
Ceres through the Houses	57
Ceres Aspects	59
Part 8: Practical Integration and Working with Ceres	**63**
Incorporating Ceres into Personal Practice	65
Guidance for Astrologers Working with Ceres	66
Part 9: Ceres, Consciousness, and the Turning of the Ages	**69**
The Unveiling of New Worlds: 1781–1807	71
Venus–Ceres–Pluto: Power, Love, and the Seeds of Revolution	72
The 1823 Conjunction at the World Point	72
Connections to the Birth of the United States	73
The Return: December 7, 2024 at 0° Aquarius	74
Part 10: The Last Harvest: Ceres, Saturn—Beginnings and Endings	**75**
Thresholds That Shape Us	77
The Anaretic Reckoning	77
My Ceres–Saturn Story	78
The Fall and the Pope	80
Closing Threads	81
What Might This Mean?	82
Part 11: Case Studies—Ceres in Living Charts	**85**
Greta Thunberg – Ceres in Aries (no accurate birth time)	87

Princess Diana – Ceres in Taurus (4th House)	87
Michelle Obama – Ceres in Sagittarius (no accurate birth time)	88
Pope Leo – Ceres in Capricorn (House Unknown)	89
Prince Harry – Ceres in Taurus (4th House)	89
Appendix A: Expanded Exercises for Working with Ceres	**91**
Releasing to Receive	93
Shamanic Journey Prompt	93
Daily Integration Practice	94
Appendix B: Ceres Keywords & Associations	**95**
Themes	97
Domains of Influence	97
Gifts of Ceres	97
Challenges of Ceres	98
Symbols & Archetypes	98
Conclusion: A Return to Sacred Care	**99**
Author's Note	**100**
Dedication	**102**
Sacred Resources & References	**103**
Sacred Sources	103
About the Author	**104**
Ceres Timeline of Archetypal Evolution	**105**

Foreword

It is becoming increasingly evident that when celestial bodies are discovered and named, their archetypes begin to emerge in the collective consciousness. Uranus was discovered amidst the French and American revolutions—times of radical change and upheaval. Neptune entered our awareness during the dawn of commercial brewing, the first drug wars, and the invention of celluloid—each linked to illusion, escapism, and altered perception. Pluto's emergence coincided with the splitting of the atom and the rise of modern psychology, both profound gateways into the unseen and the transformative. Chiron was identified just as holistic and complementary therapies began to gain traction, marking a return to integrative healing.

Although Ceres was first observed over 225 years ago, it is only in more recent decades that her archetypal presence has begun to take root in astrology and popular culture. Since the publication of the first Ceres ephemeris, themes of mothering and smothering, protection and rejection, and the deep complexity of feminine influence have come to the forefront. More importantly, Ceres has reintroduced the essential question of nurturing: how we were (or were not) nurtured, how we nurture others, how we allow others to nurture us—and crucially, how we nurture ourselves. This includes not only emotional care but also physical sustenance, such as diet, nutrition, and digestion. These concepts, once relegated to the margins, are now central to how we understand wholeness, both in astrology and in life.

I have incorporated Ceres into natal chart work for over twenty years and have often felt like a lone voice. But increasingly, others have begun to speak out—challenging inherited notions of family, gender roles, and emotional responsibility. Louise Edington is among the most fearless of these voices. With a tone that is both grounded and revolutionary, she pushes the boundaries of astrological discourse. She is almost—but not quite—a cyberpunk priestess of the stars: bold, insightful, and unapologetically feminist. If her work unsettles the old patriarchs of astrology, so be it. We need unsettling.

In this era of rapid evolution and awakening, astrology is regaining its rightful place in the cultural conversation. And Louise Edington stands at the vanguard of this transformation. Ceres in Astrology will come to be recognized as both a definitive guide and a deeply personal meditation on the archetype of nurturing. It is a timely, powerful, and much-needed contribution to modern astrology. Louise - you rock.

Steve Judd
Master Astrologer
https://www.stevejudd.co
https://www.astrobabbleproductions.com

Introduction

Why Ceres Matters Now

"Although they are only breath, words which I command are immortal."
ᴄᴡFragment 147. Sappho (7th century BCE—Greek poet, priestess of Aphrodite)

You hold in your hands a call—an invitation into deep remembrance and reconnection. Perhaps you picked this book up out of curiosity, sensing that something significant lies here, hidden in the whispers of an ancient goddess whose time has come again. Or perhaps you, like me, have sensed for a long time that something essential has been missing in our astrological understanding, something profoundly nurturing and deeply healing. That something—or rather someone—is Ceres.

Often dismissed as just a minor asteroid or dwarf planet, Ceres is, in fact, far more crucial than many astrologers recognize. Her energies permeate our personal and collective lives, quietly yet powerfully shaping our experiences of nurturing, mothering, loss, grief, attachment, and the very sustainability of life itself. When we overlook Ceres, we overlook the key to healing the profound Mother Wound that exists both within us personally and within our collective consciousness.

My journey with Ceres began unexpectedly, marked by synchronicities and deeply personal revelations that unfolded layer by layer, transforming my own understanding of motherhood, self-care, identity, and my role as an astrologer. What began as an intriguing astrological placement rapidly became a personal pilgrimage into healing and wholeness, revealing how deeply interwoven the energies of this powerful goddess are with our human stories.

This book is both personal and collective. I'll share my own story openly, inviting you into my experiences of discovery, loss, and renewal through my journey with Ceres. We will explore the deep mythological roots of this goddess, both Roman and Greek, and how those stories continue to reverberate through our individual and collective psyches today. We will also look at Ceres' astronomical discovery, her significance astrologically, and why she deserves to be embraced as a powerful personal planet equal in stature and importance to those traditionally recognized.

Beyond astrology, we'll examine how understanding Ceres can bring profound healing to our individual lives, our families, our communities, and even our planet. Her story is woven intricately with the threads of contemporary issues—climate change, displacement, attachment wounds, and societal fragmentation. Understanding and integrating the energy of Ceres is crucial not only for our personal wellbeing but for our collective future.

Finally, because astrology is also beautifully practical, I offer you a guide to understanding Ceres through the zodiac signs, providing tools and insights for working with her energy in your daily life. My intention is to empower you to embrace and integrate Ceres fully, transforming both your personal astrology practice and your understanding of the world around you.

Ceres has waited patiently for us to turn and see her clearly. Now, she is ready to speak—and to be heard.

Welcome to the sacred journey of remembering.

Welcome to Ceres.

Part 1: My Personal Journey with Ceres

The Myth, the Grain, and the Grief

All stories of the Earth begin with loss—and with the seeds that follow.

"I am she who gives the rich grain, who brings the seed to fruit and the fruit to table."
 ∞Homeric Hymn to Demeter (adapted)

"Queen of all the me, resplendent light, woman of fire, adorned with radiance—I have entered your holy temple."
 ∞Enheduanna (2285–2250 BCE—high priestess of the Moon, first known named author in history)

My Ceres Awakening

My awakening to Ceres began with a series of powerful synchronicities, sparked in September 2015 by reading *Asteroid Goddesses* by Demetra George and Douglas Bloch. At first, I was simply intrigued by her astrological symbolism—especially upon discovering that Ceres was exactly conjunct with my Ascendant at 2° Capricorn. Or so I believed.

The Hidden Mother

Around the same time, a visit from Mormon missionaries catalyzed a deeper inquiry. Two young male missionaries and their bishop had been invited into our home by one of my daughters. When I refused to let them speak to her alone, the conversation quickly turned to theology. They spoke repeatedly of the Heavenly Father, but when I asked about the Heavenly Mother, they said she was "too sacred to be spoken of"—protected, they claimed, by the Father himself.

This moment struck a deep chord. I felt the presence of a hidden feminine divine—an energy I instantly recognized as Ceres. She had been concealed, just as feminine power often is, and just as Ceres herself had long remained in the shadowy margins of astrology until her reclassification in 2006. Ironically, it also turned out that her conjunction to my Ascendant was not as exact as I thought.

The Unraveling and the Realignment

As I grew in my astrological practice, I began to question the accuracy of my birth chart. Something in me sensed the Ascendant was off. In 2020, after much reflection and using a mix of event timing, intuition, and pendulum work, I rectified my birth time. The result: I'm a Sagittarius rising, not Capricorn. The chart suddenly clicked. My rectified chart also received professional validation in 2021 from rectification astrologer Melanie Joy.

This discovery unraveled and rewove a deeper truth. My actual Ascendant is 28° Sagittarius. Ceres is at just over 3° Capricorn—now a few degrees behind, rather than exactly on, the Ascendant. That subtle shift felt like a veil lifting, both in how I understood myself and how I understood Ceres. No longer mistaken for a surface-level identity marker, she became something far more potent: a sacred influence just beneath the horizon of visibility. That too, felt true.

Threads of My Story

My life story mirrors this revelation. I am the eldest of four siblings and the only girl in a patriarchal home. My mother, who openly preferred boys, gave birth to my second brother when I was just three. The separation of 3° between my Ascendant and Ceres reflects the weight of responsibility placed on me from that point forward. Saturn, 8° past the Ascendant, echoes my father's increasing emotional and physical absence due to work and the birth of my youngest—and third—brother.

These degrees, I've since learned, can mirror developmental phases—each degree symbolizing a year or stage. Ceres and Saturn, both in Capricorn in the first house, reflect a childhood shaped by duty, self-containment, and protective instinct, yet with a Sagittarian urge for freedom. As I mothered my own children, I carried the imprint of that story—while also, both consciously and unconsciously, rewriting it.

I felt a sense of release and freedom as this shift—welcoming Ceres into her rightful place within my chart—opened a deeper understanding of my life and the hidden aspects of self I had long carried without words. I believe that uncovering a new part of the self through a previously overlooked natal placement can catalyze profound growth and evolution.

Ceres' square to my Lunar Nodes makes her what some astrologers call a "skipped step"—a soul-level lesson calling for conscious integration. That resonates deeply. I'd always been a feisty advocate for women's rights, rebelling—at least as much as I dared—against being the only sibling expected to do chores and babysit my brothers.

Just as Ceres entered our collective consciousness in 1801, bringing forth themes we'll explore throughout this book, her proximity to my Ascendant has offered deep personal healing and awakening. I began weaving her presence into every client chart, speaking about her in public presentations, and exploring the divine feminine more broadly. Her activation in my chart inspired a more intentional relationship with how my needs—physical, emotional, and spiritual—were met or unmet throughout my life. Her square to my Libra North Node in the 9th house also aligned with my exploration of feminine embodiment, sacred self-care, and higher truth.

Ceres in my chart was liberated—and in choosing to lean into her, I experienced my own liberation from old patterns and narratives. I see each planetary body as a living part of me, one I can engage with to embody its highest expression. This is the foundation of how I work with astrology, both personally and in sessions with clients and collectives. My guiding question is always: How can I partner with this part of me to grow into its fullest potential?

This journey has shaped every facet of my work. Ceres is no longer a side note or minor figure in the chart. She is a vital force. Through shamanic journeying—a form of active imagination and meditation—directed to Ceres herself, healing rituals, and years of chart exploration, I've come to know her as both archetype and ally—a living presence interwoven with my purpose.

The Offering

This book is born of that relationship. It is my offering to you: an invitation to explore your own story of mothering, being mothered, and rediscovering nourishment in all its forms. Ceres teaches us how to tend ourselves, each other, and this Earth with deeper care and reverence.

As we walk forward together into the myth, the stars, and upon the soil, may your own connection to Ceres awaken, too—and may you feel the profound healing she offers rising from the **deep roots of your life story**.

Part 2: Who Is Ceres? Understanding Her Place in Astrology

The Many Faces of Ceres

She wears many names, but always brings us back to what sustains.

Discovery and Reclassification

Ceres was first spotted on January 1, 1801, by Italian astronomer Giuseppe Piazzi at the Palermo Observatory in Sicily. Initially identifying it as a comet, Piazzi soon realized it followed a planetary orbit. With the discovery of other similar bodies soon after, astronomers created a new category—'asteroids'—coined by William Herschel in 1802. Ceres was formally classified as asteroid "1 Ceres" in 1851, and later reclassified in 2006 as a dwarf planet—alongside Pluto and Eris—by the International Astronomical Union.

Planetary Significance

Ceres stands apart within the asteroid belt between Mars and Jupiter. As the largest body in this region, she contains nearly a third of the belt's total mass. Unlike typical asteroids, Ceres has a layered interior, including a solid core and a thick mantle of water ice. Some scientists believe she may hold up to 25% water by mass—perhaps proportionally more than Earth. She even maintains a thin atmosphere and shows evidence of water vapor.

NASA Discoveries

NASA's Dawn spacecraft arrived at Ceres in 2015 and made groundbreaking discoveries, including over 130 mysterious bright spots now known to be deposits of salt and organic material—ingredients essential to life. NASA refers to her as an "embryonic planet," whose growth was disrupted by Jupiter's gravitational influence roughly four billion years ago.

The Titius-Bode Law and Planetary Alignment

Ceres' discovery was guided by the now-debated Titius-Bode Law, a mathematical formula that predicted planetary distances from the Sun. While the law later fell out of favor due to discrepancies with Neptune and Pluto, it did accurately predict Ceres' orbit at about 2.8 AU (Astronomical Units) from the Sun. That precise fit adds symbolic weight to her presence, suggesting she was once expected—then dismissed—and is now returning to reclaim her place.

A New Planetary Pairing

Her positioning also completes a meaningful trio within the personal planets. In classical astrology, the Sun and Moon are paired as core identity, Mars and Venus as desire and connection, and Mercury as the messenger. When Ceres is added as Mercury's counterpart—drawing from her pairing with Mercury in the Roman Dii Consentes, the council of twelve major gods and goddesses—we find a renewed balance. Mercury and Ceres, placed as divine siblings or counterparts in Roman cosmology, represent the bridge between mind and body, communication and care.

Ceres' connection with Mercury in this ancient divine pairing also suggests a role as a boundary-crosser—while Mercury brings messages from the gods, Ceres moves us through cycles of birth, loss, and renewal. Mercury is the innermost planet; Ceres the furthest of the personal planets. Together, they form a kind of cosmic bookend, a duality of intellect and embodiment.

Reclaiming Astrological Importance

Historically, traditional astrology marginalized Ceres, focusing on the classical planets visible to the naked eye. Planetary significance was long determined by visibility, motion, and mythic resonance—criteria that left many planetary bodies, including Ceres, in the background. But her astronomical distinction, symbolic resonance, and mythological importance suggest otherwise.

The Sacred Waters

The presence of water and organic material on Ceres connects directly to her archetype. She is the planetary body most associated with sustenance, fertility, and the nourishment of life. What could be more fitting than a celestial body holding the elemental ingredients of life itself?

A New Model for Astrology

To embrace Ceres as a personal planet is to reclaim something essential—something long ignored but deeply needed. She invites us into a more integrated model of astrology, one that honors both structure and flow, logic and intuition, body and soul.

As we'll continue to explore, her story—both astronomical and mythological—asks us to reconsider the maps we've been using, and to welcome back the wisdom of the Great Mother.

Thresholds and Time: The Evolution of Ceres

Ceres Timeline of Archetypal Evolution

This timeline offers a brief sweep through the mythic, astronomical, and collective milestones that mark Ceres' journey—from forgotten goddess to cosmic guide.

- ~9000–6000 BCE – The Great Mother appears in early agrarian cultures across Old Europe and the Near East, long before her myth is codified as Demeter.
- ~3000 BCE – Her story begins taking written shape in proto-Indo-European and early Greek traditions.
- 1801 – Ceres was 'discovered' and briefly named a planet.
- 1823 – Ceres–Venus–Pluto conjunction at 0° Aries (World Axis): a gateway moment.
- 1850s – Removed from the planetary list as smaller asteroids are discovered.
- 2006 – Reclassified as a dwarf planet the same day Pluto was demoted.
- 2024 – Ceres–Venus–Pluto conjunction at 0° Aquarius, initiating a collective reawakening.
- 2025 – 2025 – This book is born under a powerful Ceres–North Node–Saturn conjunction in Pisces: *Ceres in Astrology: Nourishment, Power, and the Rebirth of the Feminine*. A cosmic invitation to restore sacred care, ancestral memory, and collective responsibility.

PART 2: WHO IS CERES? UNDERSTANDING HER PLACE IN ASTROLOGY

Let this thread of remembrance guide you as you explore the sacred return of care, grief, nourishment, and transformation.

Part 3: Astrological Insights–Ceres as Catalyst for Consciousness

She entered the chart not as a symbol—but as a summons.

Before diving into the astrological charts themselves, it's important to understand why this exploration matters. Astrology is not just about prediction—it is about pattern recognition, symbolic language, and the evolution of meaning over time. The charts of Ceres' discovery and reclassification are not incidental; they are mythic mirrors, encoded with archetypal resonance. They mark moments when the collective was ready to receive a new facet of feminine consciousness. Let us now step into the skies of these sacred thresholds.

Ceres Discovery

Natal
Jan 1 1801, Thu
8:43 PM LMT -0:53:28
Palermo, Sicilia, Italy
Parallax
Tropical
Porphyry

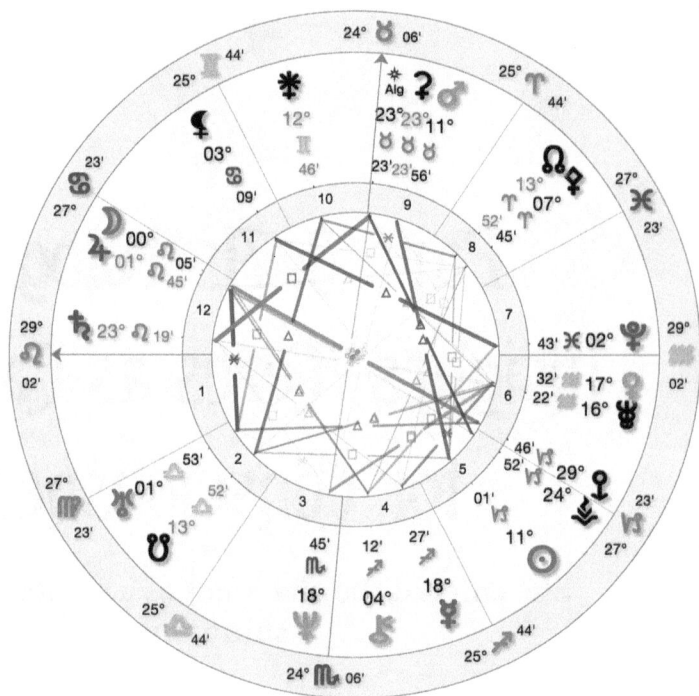

The Discovery Chart of Ceres: A Threshold Moment

Ceres was discovered on January 1, 1801, in Palermo, Italy. Her discovery chart is layered with profound symbolism. At the exact moment of her discovery, Ceres was retrograde at 23°23' Taurus—conjunct the fixed star Algol—positioned at the Midheaven, the highest and most visible point in the sky. This rare and powerful alignment unmistakably signaled her astrological importance.

Algol is often associated with Medusa and the repressed dark feminine, but this fixed star is far more than a symbol of horror or beheading. Algol speaks to the raw, untamed aspects of feminine power that have been demonized—wisdom that sees through illusion, rage that protects, cycles that renew through death and rebirth. Its presence at the Midheaven in Ceres' chart suggests that she arrived not quietly, but with a Medusan intensity that demanded recognition of all that has been shamed, hidden, or feared.

The discovery chart also reveals an exact square between Ceres and Saturn, which sat retrograde at 23°19' Leo. Saturn, the keeper of structure and patriarchal authority, in tension with Ceres, the archetype of nurture and cyclical life, mirrors the mythic tension between Demeter and Zeus. This square reflects an urgent call for humanity to reconcile nurturing and structure, softness and responsibility, grief and governance.

This theme is echoed throughout the chart. The Ascendant at 29° Leo marks an anaretic threshold degree, suggesting a collective transition from hierarchical, performative power (Leo) toward Virgo's humble, embodied service. Retrograde Jupiter at 1° Leo conjuncts the 0° Leo Moon, symbolizing the waning dominance of hierarchical authority and the rise of emotional wisdom.

The chart's North Node sits at 13° Aries in the 8th house, a potent blend of rebirth, feminine mystery (13 as the number of lunar cycles), and transformational initiation. The South Node at 13° Libra in the 2nd house suggests a past rooted in dependency on harmony and external validation—while the North Node urges courageous new beginnings in how we share resources, power, and emotional truth.

Even more striking is a rare Thor's Hammer configuration involving Neptune in Scorpio, Venus and Hygiea in Aquarius, and Black Moon Lilith in Cancer. This formation aims all its energy toward Black Moon Lilith, focusing collective attention on the reclamation of hidden, suppressed feminine power, particularly around nourishment, embodiment, and care. Neptune adds mystical depth, while Venus and Hygiea emphasize healing values through community and vision.

Please note that I use the osculating or true calculation for Black Moon Lilith as I find it the most compelling.

PART 3: ASTROLOGICAL INSIGHTS—CERES AS CATALYST FOR CONSCIOUSNESS

The Reclassification Chart: A Continuation of the Myth

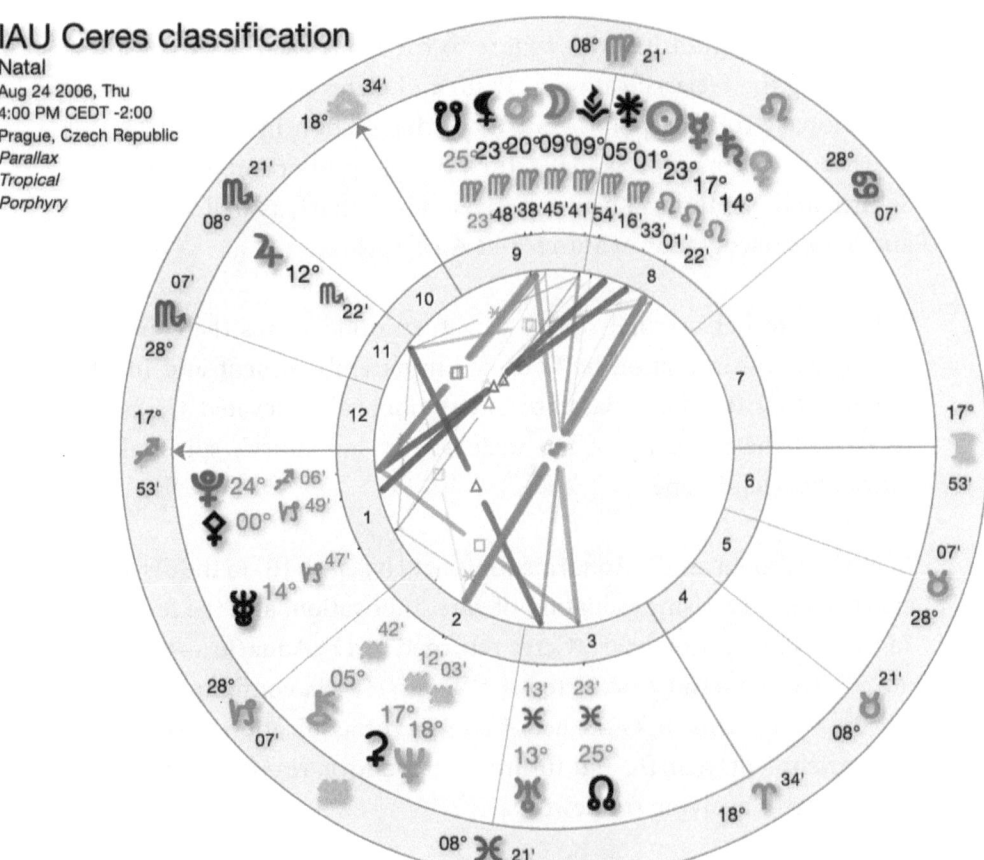

On August 24, 2006, after the discovery of Eris, Ceres was reclassified as a dwarf planet—the same day Pluto was demoted. In this chart, Ceres opposed Saturn at 17° Aquarius/Leo, emphasizing further breaking open of boundaries and challenging the hierarchical structures of society, ironically also bringing greater attempts to cling to power and control.

Ceres was also conjunct Neptune at 18° Aquarius, blurring the lines between matter and myth, and invoking a sense of spiritual reclamation.

Venus at 14° Leo, conjunct Saturn, reinforces the tension between love and limitation, beauty and control, while mirroring the deep need for the feminine to be honored within existing structures.

Pluto, at 24° Sagittarius, was square to the Nodes at 25° Virgo/Pisces, suggesting the reclassification of Pluto and Ceres together was a major evolutionary turning point. As I write this section in early 2025, this chart is experiencing a Nodal return of epic proportions, with Ceres, Saturn, and Neptune all having activated this chart, as well as Mercury and Venus retrogrades in March and April of 2025.

This echo of her original square to Saturn underscores the continued archetypal confrontation between feminine embodiment and institutional authority. The reclassification symbolically elevated Ceres and reasserted the necessity of her inclusion in humanity's spiritual and astrological landscape.

Venus' placement at 17° Aquarius conjunct Hygeia at 16° in the discovery chart reflected a rising valuation of care, innovation, and the feminine. In the reclassification chart, Ceres returned to 17° Aquarius—now conjunct Neptune—and reactivated the Venus/Hygeia configuration from her discovery. This links the act of cosmic reclassification to the values of nourishment, rebirth, and future-oriented love, reasserting her place in astrology's evolving framework.

Mercury in the 2006 reclassification chart was at 23° Leo—transiting the exact degree of Saturn in the discovery chart and square to Ceres/Algol. This Mercury placement becomes a cosmic messenger, carrying Saturn's old rules into a confrontation between old authority and Ceres' emerging, Algol-infused power. This square invites us to question who holds authority over naming, classification, and meaning—and what happens when ancient feminine wisdom rises to reclaim its voice.

Ceres and the Outer Planets: Generational Signatures

Aspects between Ceres and the outer planets—especially Pluto, Neptune, and Uranus—serve as markers of collective evolution. These configurations reflect generational shifts in how we relate to food systems, care structures, environmental consciousness, and the sacred feminine.

Pluto Generations and Ceres Themes

- Pluto in Cancer (1914–1939): A generation shaped by war, scarcity, and the breakdown of home life. Ceres themes emerge through survival-based caregiving, emphasis on family duty, and generational trauma around loss and mothering.
- Pluto in Leo (1939–1957): Raised during times of national pride and post-war growth, this generation often learned to equate worth with performance. Ceres here explores how love and care became conditional, and how creative self-expression can become a form of nurturing.
- Pluto in Virgo (1957–1972): The health-conscious revolutionaries and perfectionists. This generation brought alternative medicine, environmental movements, and holistic healing into the mainstream. Ceres in dialogue with Virgo Pluto offers devotion through service, but also confronts burnout and caretaking martyrdom.
- Pluto in Libra (1971–1984): Raised with shifting family dynamics—divorce, dual-income households—this generation grapples with fairness in relationships and shared caregiving roles. Ceres in this group seeks balance and equality in partnerships and co-parenting.

- Pluto in Scorpio (1983–1995): This generation faces deep emotional wounds, generational trauma, and themes of loss and regeneration. Ceres here uncovers powerful transformations around mothering, sexual empowerment, and taboo-breaking caregiving roles.
- Pluto in Sagittarius (1995–2008): Explorers of freedom, this generation reimagines nourishment through education, global connection, and spiritual or cultural practices. Ceres may express as a desire to redefine parenting, expand nourishment beyond the family, and revive ancestral wisdom.
- Pluto in Capricorn (2008–2024): Born into climate crisis, economic instability, and digital shifts, this group is already redefining systems. Ceres in these charts seeks sustainability, accountability, and a return to Earth-centered values in caregiving and resource-sharing.

Neptune Generations and Ceres Themes

- Neptune in Virgo (1928–1943): Emphasized order, purity, and service in the spiritual or imaginative realm. Ceres here can reflect idealized views of caregiving, but also disillusionment when nurturance does not follow a clear formula.
- Neptune in Libra (1942–1957): This generation emphasizes order, purity, and service in the spiritual or imaginative realm.
- Ceres themes include a longing for balanced relationships and beauty in the domestic sphere.
- Neptune in Scorpio (1956–1970): Deep spiritual and emotional intensity colors this generation's vision of healing and care. Ceres here may express through transformational approaches to grief, sexuality, and regenerative connection.
- Neptune in Sagittarius (1970–1984): Spiritual exploration and philosophical freedom shape this generation's relationship to parenting and nourishment. Ceres may manifest through adventurous parenting styles or intuitive learning.

- Neptune in Capricorn (1984–1998): This generation seeks to blend dreams with structure. Ceres here desires sustainable systems for care and often becomes disillusioned with institutions that fail to support the vulnerable.
- Neptune in Aquarius (1998–2012): Highly idealistic about community care, innovation, and future-oriented healing. Ceres in this generation explores collective nourishment through technology, humanitarian ideals, and non-traditional family structures.

Uranus Generations and Ceres Themes

- Uranus in Taurus (1934–1942, 2018–2026): These generations reimagine resources, nourishment, and bodily autonomy. Ceres themes emphasize sustainable innovations in food systems, ecological activism, and the rebellion of care through the body.
- Uranus in Gemini (1941–1949): This generation experiments with learning, communication, and how knowledge nurtures. Ceres here may express through unconventional education, parenting through curiosity, and mentally stimulating care.
- Uranus in Cancer (1948–1955): This generation disrupts traditional family structures and emotional expression. Ceres themes emerge in shifting maternal roles, unspoken grief, and a longing for authentic belonging.
- Uranus in Leo (1955–1962): Liberation through identity, play, and creativity defines this generation's care narrative. Ceres here nurtures through self-expression, performance, and encouraging the inner child.
- Uranus in Virgo (1961–1969): Innovations in health, routine, and service shape this generation's care models. Ceres may express through holistic healing, body wisdom, or earth-based functional nourishment.
- Uranus in Libra (1968–1975): Redefining relationships and equality in caregiving is central here. Ceres themes involve

partnership-based parenting, justice-oriented nurturance, and the balance of self and other.

- Uranus in Scorpio (1975–1981): This generation brings transformation to intimacy, power, and shadow work. Ceres in Scorpio often expresses through deep emotional bonds, trauma healing, and taboo-breaking nurturing.
- Uranus in Sagittarius (1981–1988): Freedom, exploration, and global awareness influence caregiving here. Ceres expresses through spiritual nourishment, cultural connection, and expansive approaches to education and parenting.
- Uranus in Capricorn (1988–1996): This generation questions authority and reclaims care work as essential. Ceres in Capricorn emphasizes structural reform, intergenerational responsibility, and the rebuilding of trust in systems.
- Uranus in Aquarius (1995–2003): These visionaries explore tech-integrated care, decentralization, and community innovation. Ceres themes include humanitarian nurturing, chosen family models, and the future of collective support.
- Uranus in Pisces (2003–2010): Emotional intelligence, mysticism, and spiritual caregiving define this generation's nurturing expression. Ceres here weaves intuition, compassion, and boundary-blurred connection into their care ethos.

As you can see by these themes, as Pluto, Neptune, and Uranus journey through the zodiac, Ceres dances with them, embodying each generation's lessons and gifts. These slow-moving planets define the landscape in which Ceres does her healing, remembering, and reconnection.

Ceres with Outer Planets: Example Aspects

Ceres conjunct Uranus in a generation may correlate with movements that revolutionize agriculture or parenting—like the rise of homeschooling, permaculture, or decentralized food networks.

Ceres square Pluto might describe a generation grappling with power imbalances in caregiving roles, or confronting systemic trauma around control, nourishment, and access to land or resources.

Ceres trine Neptune can show up in generations with a spiritual or idealistic view of the Earth, birth, or healing—common in the rise of holistic health movements, doula practices, or eco-spiritual communities.

Transition: From Generations to Guardianship

Having explored Ceres' presence across generations and individual charts, we now turn to her potential astrological stewardship. What does it mean for a planetary body like Ceres to hold rulership—or rather, kinship—over the signs of Taurus and Virgo? And how might her evolving dance with Venus and Pluto reshape our understanding of planetary archetypes in the years ahead?

Reimagining Rulership: Ceres, Taurus, and Virgo

While traditional astrology speaks in terms of rulership, a more fitting term for Ceres might be stewardship or kinship. Her deep resonance with Taurus is undeniable—Ceres was discovered at 23° Taurus, a powerful degree linked to embodiment and value. Taurus' earthy sensuality and affinity with food, fertility, and rhythm aligns beautifully with Ceres' archetype.

Yet Virgo, too, calls to her. The sign of sacred service, holistic care, and detailed ritual reflects Ceres' priestess qualities. Virgo embodies the wise caretaker, the one who weaves health and devotion into practical living.

In this light, Ceres may serve as co-steward of both signs, reflecting two expressions of her power: Taurus as the fertile field, and Virgo as the tender gardener.

The Symbol of Ceres

The glyph for Ceres (⚳) resembles a sickle or scythe—an ancient agricultural tool used for harvesting grain. It is composed of the **cross of matter** (the four directions, the physical world) topped by a **receptive crescent**, often seen as an **open circle** with a gap at the top. Some interpret this as a **stylized sickle**, while others see it as a **womb or vessel** that gathers what has been sown.

This symbol honors Ceres' role as a goddess of **harvest, life cycles, and sacred nourishment**. The sickle not only reaps grain, but also symbolizes the **cutting away** of what has run its course—loss, separation, and eventual rebirth.

Like all planetary symbols, Ceres' glyph is both literal and mythic. It reminds us that **true care requires tending, cutting back, and returning to the Earth.** She teaches us to honor the harvest in all its forms.

In every chart, Ceres invites us to remember that care is not a weakness—it is a cosmic intelligence. She is not an optional add-on. She is a returning necessity.

Part 4: The Mythology of Ceres and Demeter

When the grain disappears, the world forgets. When it returns, we remember who we are.

"Blessed is the one among men on Earth who has seen these things."
∽Homeric Hymn to Demeter

Ceres, the Roman goddess from whom our celestial body takes its name, embodies the fertile earth, nurturing abundance, agriculture, and maternal love. In Roman tradition, Ceres was revered not only for her bounty but also as a protector of the plebeian class, ensuring the equitable distribution of resources. Symbolically, Ceres represents the foundational nurturing principle, essential for survival and societal harmony.

Demeter, the Greek counterpart to Ceres, offers a richer, more emotionally nuanced mythology. Demeter's story is most famously depicted in the Homeric Hymn, where her beloved daughter, Persephone, is abducted by Hades, god of the underworld. Grief-stricken, Demeter withdraws her life-sustaining powers from the earth, plunging humanity into barrenness and despair. Only after Zeus intervenes is Persephone allowed to return for part of each year, symbolizing the cycle of seasons—fertility, harvest, loss, and renewal.

Comparing these myths reveals striking similarities yet nuanced differences. Both goddesses symbolize maternal nurturing, agriculture, and the life-death-rebirth cycle. However, while Ceres is primarily viewed through her beneficial societal role, Demeter's story intimately explores personal loss, grief, and the transformative power of reunion. This archetypal narrative resonates deeply with human experiences of attachment, separation, and the healing potential within cycles of grief and restoration.

These themes—loss, grief, abduction, and eventual renewal—profoundly encapsulate what we now term the "Mother Wound." This wound reflects our collective disconnection from nurturing, care, and emotional sustenance, mirrored both in personal experiences and societal structures. The abduction of Persephone symbolizes the historical diminishing of feminine power and wisdom, accelerated by the rise of patriarchal structures and further entrenched during Christianity's rise, as many feminine deities and their rites were either assimilated or suppressed.

This diminishing is also evident symbolically in architecture, art, and the collective unconscious. Ceres and Demeter have often been depicted in classical architecture and public monuments as passive or secondary figures, subtly reflecting how feminine nurturing energy has been relegated to lesser importance within societal consciousness. Yet, their persistent presence in these forms speaks to a deeply rooted collective memory and an unconscious longing for reintegration of the feminine principle into our shared reality.

By revisiting and embracing these powerful myths, we reconnect with lost wisdom, inviting a profound healing at both the personal and collective levels. Through Ceres and Demeter's enduring narratives, we recognize our own cycles of loss and recovery and are invited into deeper intimacy with the archetypal feminine—essential not only for our individual wholeness but for the healing of our world.

Ceres, Excess, and the Cry for Redemption

Astrologer **Dawn Bodrogi** once described her first encounter with Ceres not through astrology, but through literature—specifically a passage from *The Brothers Karamazov*, in which a tormented character recites lines from Friedrich Schiller's *Hymn to Joy*. The poem describes Ceres descending from Olympus to search for her daughter, only to find a world steeped in violence, greed, and degradation. A world that has abandoned the rhythms of nature—and with them, the divine feminine.

> *From the peak of high Olympus*
> *Came the mother Ceres down,*
> *Seeking in those savage regions*
> *Her lost daughter Proserpine . . .*
>
> *But the Goddess found no refuge,*
> *Found no kindly welcome there,*
> *And no temple bearing witness*
> *To the worship of the gods . . .*

The poem, as Bodrogi reflected, speaks to a world in need of redemption—not just spiritual or moral, but ecological. When we abandon the balance of Earth's rhythms, we abandon ourselves. When we neglect the nourishment and restraint symbolized by Ceres, we invite chaos, excess, and collapse.

> *Would he purge his soul from vileness*
> *And attain to light and worth,*
> *He must turn and cling forever*
> *To his ancient Mother Earth . . .*

Bodrogi wrote:

"Where Ceres lies in the chart, we have hungers we must acknowledge, or they may destroy us."

This invocation of Ceres is not sentimental. It is mythic and moral. She is not simply the goddess of harvest—she is the reckoner of balance, the witness to excess, and the Earth herself demanding we return to her with reverence.

Part 5: Archetypal and Psychological Significance

"You are she who creates the seed of the people, the breath of life is yours."
∽Enheduanna (2285–2250 BCE—high priestess of the Moon, first known named author in history)

Astrologically, Ceres represents profound archetypal and psychological energies rooted deeply in the human psyche. To understand her fully is to journey through rich archetypal landscapes, exploring not only the nurturing maternal principle but also how we experience attachment, loss, and healing. Through the lenses of Jungian psychology, attachment theory, Internal Family Systems, and quantum consciousness, Ceres emerges as a powerful symbol guiding us toward personal and collective integration.

The Archetypes of Ceres: The Mother's Many Faces

Ceres embodies the archetypal Mother in all her complexity, far beyond simplistic notions of nurturing alone. She reveals the multifaceted expressions of mothering, each holding potent gifts and potential shadows:

- **The Loving Mother:** Providing warmth, nourishment, safety, and unconditional acceptance. Astrologically, well-integrated Ceres energy encourages healthy bonds, emotional security, and abundant self-nurturing.
- **The Devouring or Smothering Mother:** Reflecting over-protection, dependency, control, or emotional enmeshment. Astrologically, challenging aspects to Ceres can manifest in issues around boundaries, autonomy, and emotional manipulation.
- **The Absent or Detached Mother:** Symbolizing emotional neglect, absence, or withholding of affection and nurturance, causing deep inner wounds around self-worth and self-care. Difficult placements of Ceres may indicate themes of abandonment or emotional isolation.
- **The Helicopter Mother:** Manifesting as anxious hovering, excessive control, or over-involvement—stemming from fear of loss or harm. Here, Ceres may point to issues around trust, autonomy, and emotional security.

- **The Grieving Mother:** The profound grief of Demeter's loss of Persephone symbolically reflects the archetypal experiences of attachment and inevitable separation. Astrologically, Ceres placements may indicate themes of loss, grief, and subsequent renewal.

In astrological practice, exploring these archetypal faces of Ceres helps illuminate our individual patterns of nurturing, emotional attachment, and maternal wounding, guiding us toward greater self-awareness, compassion, and healing.

Mother Wound and Attachment Theory

Central to Ceres' mythology is the "Mother Wound"—a deep, primal wound around nurturing, connection, and emotional security. Psychologically, this wound originates from our earliest experiences of care, nourishment, and emotional attunement—or their painful absence. Attachment theory clearly mirrors these themes, exploring how early relational patterns with primary caregivers shape our capacity for intimacy, trust, and emotional connection throughout life.

Secure attachment is nurtured by consistent, loving responsiveness (healthy Ceres expression), while insecure attachment styles (anxious, avoidant, disorganized) often emerge from disrupted nurturing—overbearing, inconsistent, or neglectful. Astrologically, Ceres placements can reveal our attachment wounds and guide us toward understanding and healing these deep-seated patterns.

Working consciously with Ceres through attachment theory supports a profound shift toward secure attachment patterns—transforming our capacity to nourish and be nourished emotionally, relationally, and spiritually.

Part 5: Archetypal and Psychological Significance

Psychological Depth: Jungian Insights and Internal Family Systems (IFS)

From a Jungian perspective, Ceres represents a vital facet of the feminine archetype, embodying the Great Mother—the universal, nurturing principle capable of profound creation and profound destruction. Jung taught that integrating these complex archetypal energies within ourselves leads to psychological wholeness or "individuation."

Astrologically, Ceres placements highlight where we must reclaim fragmented aspects of this nurturing feminine energy within ourselves, integrating shadow elements such as loss, grief, dependency, or control into conscious awareness, thus fostering wholeness and authentic self-care.

Internal Family Systems (IFS), another potent psychological model, offers profound insights into working with Ceres archetypally. IFS views the psyche as composed of subpersonalities or "parts," each holding unique wounds, needs, and roles. From an IFS lens, the Mother archetype represented by Ceres can manifest as various inner parts—protective managers (controlling, perfectionistic), wounded exiles (abandoned, needy), or firefighters (impulsive, self-destructive).

Through astrological insight and compassionate inner dialogue, working with Ceres can facilitate deep internal healing, restoring harmony among these inner parts and nurturing inner coherence, self-leadership, and psychological resilience.

Quantum, Energetic, and Archetypal Healing: Inner to Outer Integration

Finally, exploring Ceres through a quantum, energetic, and archetypal perspective invites us into a deeply interconnected understanding of healing—one where inner psychological integration directly contributes to outer collective transformation.

Quantum theories propose that our internal states resonate outwardly, influencing collective fields energetically. Ceres' archetypal themes of nurturing, interconnectedness, and cyclical renewal deeply embody this quantum reality. Healing the Mother Wound within ourselves contributes powerfully to the collective healing of emotional, social, and ecological wounds in the world around us.

Astrologically, consciously engaging with Ceres initiates energetic shifts—on personal, relational, and societal levels—where individual reclamation of suppressed nurturing energies ripple outward, supporting collective transformation toward greater emotional maturity, ecological stewardship, and compassionate interdependence.

Thus, Ceres' astrology is not merely personal—it is profoundly transpersonal, symbolic of humanity's broader evolutionary journey toward wholeness, balance, and collective renewal.

Part 6: Ceres in Our Collective Evolution

She doesn't just visit generations—she reweaves them.

Ceres and the Industrial Revolution

Ceres' symbolism is profoundly intertwined with humanity's relationship to nourishment, land, and resources—relationships that shifted dramatically during the Industrial Revolution. This period of rapid technological advancement, mechanization, and industrial-scale agriculture profoundly altered our collective connection to Earth. Humanity's growing disconnection from natural cycles, embodied care, and sustainable practices mirrors the mythological separation Ceres endured from her beloved Persephone. Industrialization, while bringing many societal benefits, also fostered widespread estrangement from the intimate, reciprocal relationships once held with the Earth, giving rise to environmental degradation, exploitation, and a distorted sense of dominion over nature.

Climate Crisis, Displacement, and Refugee Crises: Modern Manifestations of Ceres

Today, Ceres speaks urgently through the global climate crisis, refugee movements, and ecological displacement. These issues echo her ancient myth of loss and searching—a mother grieving her abducted daughter, symbolizing humanity's disconnection from Earth's wisdom and care. Climate change, driven by ecological neglect and unsustainable resource extraction, uproots entire communities, mirroring Persephone's descent into the underworld and the resulting barrenness that gripped the world. Refugee crises, environmental displacement, and food scarcity embody modern-day Persephone experiences, requiring a profound collective reconnection and nurturing response reflective of Ceres' essence.

Societal Disconnection Mirroring Personal Disconnection

On a deeper, symbolic level, our societal disconnection from the nurturing, mothering principle reflects personal and collective estrangement from inner nourishment. The growing disconnection from embodied wisdom and sustainable living patterns parallels individual estrangement from emotional nurturance, care, and the ability to hold oneself and others in tenderness. This alienation manifests in increased mental health challenges, emotional exhaustion, and an epidemic of loneliness and isolation, mirroring the drought and emotional barrenness depicted in Ceres' myth.

A Vision for Healing Through Ceres Consciousness

Healing through Ceres consciousness involves reawakening to our inherent interconnectedness with the Earth and reclaiming collective responsibility to steward its resources with reverence. It calls for a return to sustainable practices rooted in mutual respect and reciprocity—embodying a renewed commitment to ecological, emotional, and social nourishment. Ceres invites us into transformative actions: regenerative agriculture, eco-friendly urban planning, community-based care, equitable resource distribution, and policies that honor human dignity and planetary health.

By embracing Ceres consciousness, we reestablish sacred reciprocity between humanity and the Earth, shifting from exploitation to stewardship, from disconnection to deep relational healing. This collective shift, mirrored in our personal lives, invites a powerful reconnection with nourishment in all forms, restoring balance, abundance, and vitality to our shared planetary home.

Part 7: Working with Ceres in Your Natal Chart

To find her, follow the ache. Then follow the root.

Like all planetary beings, Ceres' placement by sign, house, and aspect colors how her themes emerge in the birth chart. Her energy weaves through the fabric of our lived experience, particularly in how we nurture and are nurtured, how we relate to the Earth, and how we cycle through loss, renewal, and abundance.

Understanding Ceres by Sign, House, and Aspect

For example, my own Ceres is in Capricorn in the first house, only 4° from my 28° Sagittarius Ascendant, conjunct natal Saturn in Capricorn and square to the natal Lunar Nodes. My mother was alone when I was born—a reflection of the norms of the time and place—and I was soon followed by three younger brothers within seven years. Responsibility was placed on my shoulders from a young age; I was not breastfed, was expected to help "mother" my siblings, and physical affection was limited. Themes of responsibility, restriction, self-reliance, and isolation—all Capricornian qualities—are clearly reflected in this early Ceres imprint.

Later in life, aging and elderhood wove themselves into my story. I became a mother at 37 and 40, moving toward the polarity point in Cancer. As a mother, I emphasized physical affection, breastfed long-term, and even led home birth groups, birthing my youngest child at home in a birthing pool. I devoted myself completely to mothering—a healing and balancing act between the Capricornian and Cancerian expressions within me.

My disciplined approach to nurturing my physical and emotional needs also reflects the Capricorn signature. Over time, Ceres' placement has revealed itself as both wound and gift—a map of healing as much as a record of origin.

Ceres as Wound and Gift

The blending of planet, sign, and house matters profoundly. Many with more challenging placements may find themselves naturally gravitating toward the opposite polarity—seeking to balance the scales within themselves and their relationships.

Ceres' expression is further shaped by her aspects with other planets. Challenging aspects may indicate areas where giving and receiving nurturing feels strained, potentially manifesting as difficulties with food, caregiving, emotional vulnerability, or feelings of abandonment. Yet within these struggles lies the sacred opportunity for healing and integration.

Conversely, harmonious aspects to Ceres often speak to a natural gift for nurturing others and oneself, a strong affinity with nature, and a profound respect for cycles of life and renewal. When well-supported, Ceres can offer a stable, sustaining presence, one rooted deeply in the rhythms of the Earth and the wisdom of unconditional care.

The placement of Ceres by sign, house, and planetary relationship offers rich insights into how themes of nourishment, loss, caregiving, fertility, and earth stewardship unfold in a lifetime.

Keywords for Ceres, the signs, and the houses are invaluable tools in exploring her meaning. Attuning to how these words resonate within your own life story—and reflecting on your early experiences of nurturing—can deepen your understanding of this potent, often overlooked archetype.

Here is a comprehensive list of keywords to guide your exploration. The next chapter will offer a brief breakdown of Ceres through the signs, but remember: your Ceres is a living, breathing energy within you, and her full meaning will reveal itself through your personal dance with her themes.

Keywords for Ceres:

- Food
- Agriculture
- Harvest
- Earth stewardship
- Money and material security
- Renewal and rebirth
- Relationship to food and nourishment
- Connection with the physical world
- Nurturing (giving and receiving)
- Mother wound
- Transitional phases in a woman's life (maiden, mother, crone)
- Fertility and cycles
- Abundance and sustainability
- Family and caregiving dynamics
- Simplicity and natural living
- "Good for you" choices
- Strong desire to nurture and protect
- Respect and reverence for all living beings
- Grief, loss, and separation
- Destruction and rebuilding
- Time-sharing and caretaking
- Democratic, inclusive love
- Environmental and nutritional consciousness
- Understated elegance
- Appreciation for the ordinary and sacred in daily life
- Tending to the garden of life—literal and metaphorical
- Holistic healing and body wisdom
- Devotion to the rhythms of nature

Ceres calls us back to what is natural, whole, and life-sustaining—within ourselves, within each other, and within the world around us.

Practical Reflections and Chart Examples

A person with Ceres square Saturn may experience themes of early deprivation, emotional neglect, or rigid conditioning around how care was given or withheld. Over time, this placement can mature into strong boundaries and a deeply responsible caregiving style.

Someone with Ceres trine the Moon may find nurturing comes naturally—both giving and receiving care flows with ease, often supported by positive maternal experiences or a strong intuitive connection to others' needs.

Ceres conjunct Pluto in a natal chart can suggest transformational experiences around motherhood, loss, or deep soul-level grief that eventually give rise to powerful healing abilities and regeneration.

These signatures offer not only insight into individual life paths, but also highlight how our personal experiences of care are shaped within larger cultural and evolutionary arcs. Ceres shows us that the deeply personal is always, in some way, profoundly collective.

Your Ceres Questions

To apply these generational insights, begin by locating Ceres in your natal chart by **sign, house, and aspect**. Then reflect:

- What does this placement reveal about how I give and receive care?

- What ancestral or collective patterns might I be carrying around nourishment, loss, or protection?
- How might I restore balance in my relationship with the Earth, my body, and the feminine within?
- Are there outer planet connections suggesting a generational or archetypal role I am here to integrate?

Meditate on how your personal Ceres story intersects with the generational arc you're part of. This is the invitation of Ceres: to root your healing in the soul of the world.

NOTE FOR THE READER
To view your natal chart with Ceres included, you can use online astrology tools such as Astro.com or Astro-Seek.com. Make sure to select "Ceres" from the list of additional objects before generating your chart.

For deeper insight, you may wish to consult a professional astrologer who works with Ceres.

Transition: From Generations to Guardianship

Having explored Ceres' presence across generations and individual charts, we now turn to her potential astrological stewardship. What does it mean for a planetary body like Ceres to hold rulership—or rather, kinship—over the signs of Taurus and Virgo? And how might her evolving dance with Venus and Pluto reshape our understanding of planetary archetypes in the years ahead?

Reimagining Rulership: Ceres, Taurus, and Virgo

While traditional astrology speaks in terms of rulership, a more fitting term for Ceres might be stewardship or kinship. Her deep resonance with Taurus is undeniable—Ceres was discovered at 23° Taurus, a powerful degree linked to embodiment and value. Taurus' earthy sensuality and affinity with food, fertility, and rhythm aligns beautifully with Ceres' archetype.

Yet Virgo, too, calls to her. The sign of sacred service, holistic care, and detailed ritual reflects Ceres' priestess qualities. Virgo embodies the wise caretaker, the one who weaves health and devotion into practical living. In this light, Ceres may serve as co-steward of both signs, reflecting two expressions of her power: Taurus as the fertile field, and Virgo as the tender gardener.

In every chart, Ceres invites us to remember that care is not a weakness—it is a cosmic intelligence. She is not an optional add-on. She is a returning necessity."

Ceres through the Signs, Houses, and Aspects

Building upon the foundational understanding of Ceres' role in the chart, this section offers brief yet rich descriptions of her placement through the zodiac signs, the houses, and aspect blending. These interpretations emphasize self-care, nurturing needs, mother wound healing, and empowerment, helping you access the deeper gifts Ceres offers within you.

PART 7: WORKING WITH CERES IN YOUR NATAL CHART

Ceres through the Signs

Building upon the foundational understanding of Ceres' role in the chart, this section offers brief yet rich descriptions of her placement through the zodiac signs. These interpretations emphasize self-care, nurturing needs, mother wound healing, and empowerment, helping you access the deeper gifts Ceres offers within you.

- Ceres in Aries Nurture through independence, bravery, and physical action. Healing the mother wound involves reclaiming your right to exist boldly and assertively. Physical movement, solo adventures, and initiating projects nourish your spirit. Learning to self-validate is key.
- Ceres in Taurus Find nourishment in sensory experiences, nature, and material stability. Healing emerges through reconnecting with your body, self-worth, and the abundance around you. Slow rituals, gardening, cooking, and tending to comfort and security are essential acts of self-care.
- Ceres in Gemini Care is found through communication, curiosity, and learning. Healing the mother wound involves reclaiming your voice, staying mentally agile, and nurturing diverse connections. Sharing stories, teaching, writing, and playful conversations feed your soul.
- Ceres in Cancer Nurture comes through emotional intimacy, creating safe spaces, and caregiving. Healing involves establishing healthy emotional boundaries and embracing both the giving and receiving of deep care. Home, family, tradition, and honoring ancestral roots strengthen your spirit.
- Ceres in Leo Nurture through creativity, celebration, and self-recognition. Healing the mother wound means reclaiming your inherent right to shine, to be seen, and to take pride in your being. Creative projects, leadership, and joyful self-expression are essential nourishment.

- Ceres in Virgo Find nourishment in organization, holistic service, and tending to daily rhythms. Healing comes by embracing imperfection, cultivating self-compassion, and viewing service as sacred. Rituals of body care, craftsmanship, and devotion to meaningful tasks replenish you.
- Ceres in Libra Care flows through creating beauty, harmony, and equitable relationships. Healing involves finding balance between self and other, asserting your own needs while fostering mutual nurturance. Art, diplomacy, design, and partnership enrich your nurturing capacities.
- Ceres in Scorpio Nurture comes through emotional truth, intimacy, and transformation. Healing the mother wound involves allowing vulnerability, trusting others carefully, and embracing emotional regeneration. Shadow work, deep emotional bonds, and profound loyalty are pathways to empowerment.
- Ceres in Sagittarius Nurture through freedom, adventure, learning, and faith. Healing involves reclaiming optimism, a broader vision of life, and permission to expand beyond imposed limitations. Travel, philosophy, storytelling, and connecting with diverse cultures nourish your spirit.
- Ceres in Capricorn Find nourishment in structure, achievement, and honoring responsibility with compassion. Healing involves redefining success to include emotional and physical wellbeing, allowing vulnerability within strength. Building sustainable foundations, mentoring, and long-term goals restore your sense of purpose.
- Ceres in Aquarius Care flows through innovation, authenticity, and communal connection. Healing the mother wound means honoring your uniqueness, valuing diverse communities, and nurturing collective visions. Technology, activism, visionary work, and friendship networks feed your heart.
- Ceres in Pisces Nurture comes through spiritual practice, compassion, creativity, and surrender to the unseen. Healing involves setting healthy emotional boundaries while embracing

sensitivity as a gift. Music, art, meditation, healing arts, and sacred dreaming nourish your essence.

In each sign, Ceres shows a pathway back to the sacred cycles of nourishment, connection, and renewal. Her wisdom invites us to tend both ourselves and the world around us with conscious, loving care.

Ceres through the Houses

Where Ceres falls by house in your natal chart reveals the area of life where you're invited to nourish and be nourished—where the sacred cycle of giving and receiving care plays out most intimately.

- Ceres in the 1st House Nurture begins with your identity, body, and presence in the world. You may be seen as a caregiver or protector, but must also learn to feed yourself first. Personal confidence and autonomy are essential to your wellbeing.
- Ceres in the 2nd House Find nourishment in physical resources, self-worth, and stability. You are deeply attuned to the material world and gain comfort through beauty, nature, and touch. Healing may involve rewriting early messages around value and support.
- Ceres in the 3rd House Care flows through words, connection, and learning. You nurture others with your voice or listening ear. Healing involves reclaiming your mental space and speaking your truth with clarity.
- Ceres in the 4th House Nurture arises from rootedness, ancestry, and emotional safety. You may carry deep generational caregiving roles or wounds. Healing involves tending to your inner child and creating a sanctuary-like home within and without.
- Ceres in the 5th House Nourishment expresses through creativity, play, and joy. You may mother through artistic

expression, teaching, or encouraging others to shine. Healing involves allowing pleasure and validating your inner light.
- Ceres in the 6th House Care comes through daily rituals, service, and healing. You nourish others through work, wellness, or acts of devotion. Healing the mother wound means releasing perfectionism and honoring your limits.
- Ceres in the 7th House Care is found in relationships and one-on-one bonds. There may be themes of co-dependency or healing through partnership. True care arises when mutual support and balance are honored.
- Ceres in the 8th House Nurture deepens through intimacy, emotional truth, and shared resources. There may be experiences of loss that shape how you give and receive care. Transformation is your gift.
- Ceres in the 9th House Find nourishment through teaching, travel, philosophy, and belief. You care by sharing your perspective and expanding others' horizons. Healing involves claiming the right to explore your truth and grow your spirit.
- Ceres in the 10th House Care flows into public roles—teacher, leader, guide. You may feel pressure to "perform" caregiving or succeed in nurturing roles. Healing involves allowing softness within strength and redefining what it means to lead.
- Ceres in the 11th House Nurture radiates through community, friendship, and shared visions. You build networks, movements, or collective support systems. Healing involves receiving support in return.
- Ceres in the 12th House Care emerges through compassion, spiritual practice, and intuitive empathy. You may feel others' needs deeply. Healing comes through rest, ritual, and releasing martyr patterns to rediscover soulful renewal.

Ceres Aspects

To deepen your relationship with Ceres in both natal and transiting charts, it's helpful to explore how she interacts with other planetary archetypes. These combinations reveal the nuances of how we nurture, protect, grieve, and grow—and they offer a more embodied and relational view of our astrological story.

Use the following section as a springboard. Whether you're looking at your natal chart, a client's, or current transits, allow these archetypal blends to guide intuitive insight. Pay attention to patterns that emerge, and how Ceres may be inviting new forms of care, reclamation, or healing.

- Ceres–Sun: When Ceres meets the Sun, our identity and vitality are shaped by how we give and receive nourishment. This may reflect strong maternal figures, or a calling to embody nurturing in a visible, life-guiding way.
- Ceres–Moon: Emotional security and care are central. These aspects often reveal early childhood patterns around food, mothering, and emotional attunement. Healing often comes through reparenting or reconnecting with ancestral rhythms.
- Ceres–Mercury: Communication becomes a vehicle for nurturing. These people may soothe through words, teach about nourishment, or write from a place of deep caregiving wisdom. Transits can bring news or messages related to family or health.
- Ceres–Venus: This pairing blends beauty, love, and devotion. There may be a sensual, embodied way of loving, or a desire to care through aesthetics, touch, or ritual. These aspects may also explore the intersection of self-worth and care.
- Ceres–Mars: Care takes action here—protective, fierce, and determined. These individuals often fight for others, champion

causes of food justice, or assertively tend to those they love. Transits can initiate passionate efforts to restore balance or defend what's sacred.

- Ceres–Jupiter: Generosity of spirit and expansive mothering themes arise. These aspects might suggest a natural teacher or a hunger for meaning through service. Transits may trigger philosophical shifts around nourishment or beliefs about abundance.
- Ceres–Saturn: This combination can reflect themes of restriction or responsibility in caregiving. There may be early deprivation that eventually ripens into deeply reliable stewardship. Lessons of boundaries, discipline, and sustainable care abound.
- Ceres–Uranus: Nurturing becomes innovative, unconventional, or erratic. These aspects often call for new paradigms in care—radical inclusion, neurodivergent needs, or eco-futurist visions. Transits can shock the system into reimagining what care looks like.
- Ceres–Neptune: Spiritual and intuitive caregiving. This pairing can reflect visionary empathy or escapist tendencies around responsibility. Dreams and mysticism often carry messages of healing through devotion and softness.
- Ceres–Pluto: Deep, transformative caregiving themes arise—grief, rebirth, and soul-level regeneration. These aspects often mark profound losses or powerful healing experiences tied to motherhood, trauma, or the Earth herself.
- Ceres–Chiron: The wound and the remedy meet. This aspect can reflect pain around abandonment, unmet needs, or failed care—but also holds the potential for profound healing when care is extended with compassion and consciousness.
- Ceres–North/South Nodes: These points show karmic patterns around care and evolution through nourishment. Ceres on the North Node urges us forward into healing service; on the South Node, she may hold ancestral gifts or unresolved maternal stories.

PART 7: WORKING WITH CERES IN YOUR NATAL CHART

These combinations are not exhaustive, but they offer portals for reflection. You are encouraged to blend them, follow your intuition, and notice how Ceres is speaking uniquely in each chart you touch.

Part 8: Practical Integration and Working with Ceres

This work is sacred, messy, and cyclical. Just like the Earth.

Ceres invites not just intellectual understanding but practical, embodied integration. Her wisdom becomes most powerful when lived. This section offers pathways for working consciously with Ceres energy in daily life, through personal practices and astrological consultations.

Incorporating Ceres into Personal Practice

Rituals:

- Create simple rituals tied to Earth cycles: honoring the equinoxes, celebrating harvests, planting seeds with intention.
- Light a candle at mealtimes to offer gratitude for nourishment.

Meditations:

- Visualize being cradled by the Earth, supported by its steady, nourishing presence.
- Journey inward to meet your inner mother archetype—what does she look like, say, or offer you?

Journaling Prompts:

- How was I nurtured as a child, and how do I nurture myself now?
- Where do I feel abundant and cared for? Where do I feel lacking?
- How do I embody the cycles of giving and receiving in my life?

Shamanic Journeys:

- Journey to meet Ceres herself, asking her to show you how to reclaim nourishment, care, or connection with the natural world.
- Explore the inner landscape of your "harvest"—what in your life is ripe, ready, or in need of tending?

Healing Exercises:

- Practice grounding techniques, connecting consciously with the Earth (barefoot walking, gardening, tending to houseplants).
- Engage in somatic practices that honor body wisdom and physical care (yoga, dance, breathwork).
- Create a "nourishment altar" with objects representing what feeds your spirit.

Guidance for Astrologers Working with Ceres

When interpreting Ceres in a client's chart:

- Approach with tenderness, as Ceres often highlights vulnerable themes of nurturing, abandonment, loss, and repair.
- Explore the client's early caregiving environment with sensitivity—listen for both grief and resilience.
- Use Ceres placement to illuminate how a client can better nourish themselves and others.
- Honor Ceres' broader role: not just "mothering" but stewardship of all life. Help clients connect with environmental causes, community care, and earth-centered rituals if appropriate.

Part 8: Practical Integration and Working with Ceres

- Encourage reflection on both wounding and empowerment: where healing the nurturing principle can lead to profound personal and collective evolution.

By consciously working with Ceres, we root ourselves more deeply in the sacred cycles of nourishment, loss, healing, and renewal. Her wisdom invites not only personal healing but a reconnection to the larger web of life that sustains us all.

Part 9: Ceres, Consciousness, and the Turning of the Ages

Ceres holds the thread between collapse and care.

What is honored is cultivated. What is cultivated endures.

Although this book does not dive deeply into the full synodic or return cycles of Ceres, we must acknowledge her place in the greater unfolding of celestial consciousness. The timing of her discovery, and her presence in significant historical and cosmic conjunctions, points to a deeper narrative that is still unfolding—one in which Ceres plays a vital role.

The Unveiling of New Worlds: 1781-1807

The discovery of Uranus in 1781 shattered the limits of classical astrology, breaking open the heavens beyond Saturn. It marked the beginning of a new epoch of consciousness—one that invited humanity to think beyond what was previously visible. In the decades that followed, the celestial feminine emerged:

- Ceres was discovered in 1801.
- Pallas Athena in 1802.
- Juno in 1804.
- Vesta in 1807.

This wave of discovery signaled a rising awareness of the divine feminine in her many faces—nurturer, strategist, partner, and keeper of the flame. After this flurry, no major planetary bodies were added to the astrological lexicon until Neptune's discovery in 1846.

Venus-Ceres-Pluto: Power, Love, and the Seeds of Revolution

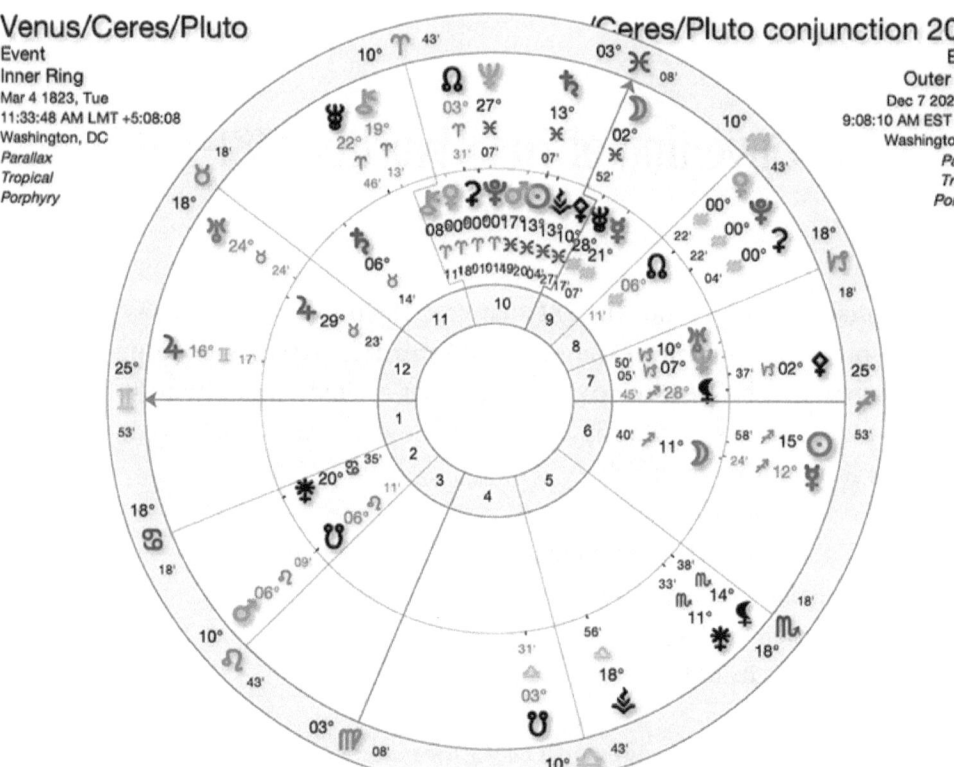

The 1823 Conjunction at the World Point

On March 4, 1823, Venus, Ceres, and Pluto formed a rare triple conjunction at 0° Aries—the very beginning of the zodiac, also known as the world axis or point of creation.

- Ceres and Pluto were conjunct within one arc minute at 0°01' Aries.
- Venus was just behind at 0°18' Aries.

This moment was mythically and astrologically profound. Venus, Ceres, and Pluto—three archetypes connected by the Persephone myth—met at the point of initiation. This triple conjunction can be seen as a symbolic birth point of a new collective evolutionary thread, rooted in the reclamation and reintegration of the feminine principle through the cycles of desire, nourishment, death, and rebirth.

These three can be seen as an energetic triad: maiden (Venus), mother (Ceres), and crone (Pluto), or youth, adult, and elder. Each represents a stage of transformation and embodiment:

- Venus as desire, love, the spark of life.
- Ceres as nurturance, loss, and cyclical renewal.
- Pluto as death, transformation, and soul-level evolution.

It is also worth noting that Ceres and Pluto were reclassified together as dwarf planets in 2006—a symbolic recognition of their shared importance in our solar story.

Connections to the Birth of the United States

This conjunction took place just 34 years after the U.S. Constitution went into effect on March 4, 1789—a date that now echoes in the sky through this cosmic alignment. At the time of the 1823 conjunction:

- The transiting lunar nodes were at 6° Leo (South Node) and 6° Aquarius (North Node), forming a reverse nodal return to the 1776 U.S. chart.
- Saturn sat at 6° Taurus, squaring the nodal axis and reflecting the Saturn–Ceres square present in Ceres' discovery chart.
- The Moon was at 11°40′ Sagittarius—closely conjunct the Sibly chart Ascendant at 12° Sagittarius.

These alignments suggest that the Ceres–Pluto–Venus conjunction was not just a new beginning for the collective, but deeply tied to the soul and destiny of the United States. The country, born in the fires of revolution and idealism, was beginning to reckon with themes of power, nurture, sovereignty, and transformation.

The Return: December 7, 2024 at 0° Aquarius

After over 200 years, Venus, Ceres, and Pluto once again meet—this time at 0° Aquarius, another critical point of profound symbolic weight. This upcoming conjunction arrives on the heels of several significant alignments at this degree:

- Mar 31, 2020: Mars/Saturn conjunction
- Dec 21, 2020: Jupiter/Saturn conjunction ("Great Mutation" into the Air Element)
- Mar 6, 2022: Venus/Mars conjunction
- Jan 20, 2024: Sun and Pluto ingress 0° Aquarius
- Feb 5, 2024: Mercury/Pluto conjunction
- Feb 14, 2024: Mars/Pluto conjunction
- Feb 17, 2024: Venus/Pluto conjunction

This concentrated activation of 0° Aquarius signals a major threshold in human consciousness. The triple conjunction of Venus, Ceres, and Pluto at this degree may represent a rebirth of feminine power—no longer hidden, divided, or diminished, but integrated, sovereign, and visionary.

Aquarius speaks to collective evolution, liberation, technology, and new paradigms. As we step into the Age of Air—distinct from the astrological Age of Aquarius, but aligned with its symbolic themes—we are invited to carry forward what was seeded at 0° Aries in 1823 and birth it anew through Aquarian vision.

Part 10: The Last Harvest: Ceres, Saturn—Beginnings and Endings

Not every cycle needs to bloom again.

There comes a time when even the soil must rest. And from that stillness, begin again.

Thresholds That Shape Us

There are degrees in astrology that act like cosmic switchbacks—places where the spiral of evolution turns sharply and requires us to reorient. **0°** and **29°** are two of those places. The beginning and the end. The inhale and the exhale. The spark and the surrender.

When planets pass through these degrees, the energy is heightened, pressured, potent. And when those planets are Ceres and Saturn—symbols of care and control, harvest and restriction, the nurturer and the builder—their contact at the final degree of the zodiac becomes more than just a transit. It becomes an initiation.

Pisces is the last sign in the zodiac. 29° Pisces is the final ripple in the great cosmic sea—where karma dissolves and structures dissolve with it. It is the place where we return what isn't ours to carry. Where we weep for what never was. Where we let go.

The Anaretic Reckoning

On **May 13, 2025, Ceres and Saturn conjoined at 29° Pisces**—the very end of the zodiac. It is not a beginning. It is a reckoning.

These two met before, not kindly. In **Ceres' discovery chart**, they formed a tense square. In her reclassification chart, they opposed one another—locked in a power struggle.

Control over care. Authority over the feminine. Structure without nurture. Harvest without rest.

Now, at the threshold of Pisces, they come together not in battle, but in weary recognition. Something must end. Something must be composted. Something must be released.

Not every cycle needs to bloom again.

My Ceres-Saturn Story

As I complete the birthing of this book on the May 13th, 2025 Ceres-Saturn conjunction, I feel compelled to share where I am in my evolving journey with Ceres.

I was born with **Ceres conjunct Saturn**—the goddess of nourishment fused with the god of structure, form, and sometimes, absence.

And like all things in astrology, it isn't just metaphor. It's my lived experience.

My father died in 1997.

And now, decades later, as I complete the writing of this book I've planned a visit back to England—back to the land that shaped me, back to the roots that, I thought, might still hold something.

But two days before writing this, I learned my mother will be away during our visit.

Part 10: The Last Harvest: Ceres, Saturn—Beginnings and Endings

Gone.

Just like that.

And my three brothers? They've responded with silence, disinterest, or surface-level civility.

No one seems particularly moved that we're coming.

I'm not surprised.

But I am . . . stung.

There's a part of me—the old me—that wants to justify it.

"That's just how they are."

"They don't know how to show up emotionally."

"They're busy."

But the truth is simpler.

And harder.

They don't see me.

Maybe they never did.

And in that realization, something ancient inside me lets go.

This is the *Ceres–Saturn initiation*: The ache of reaching out with open arms . . . and finding no one there to meet you.

The betrayal of absence.

The abandonment that isn't loud or dramatic—just consistent. Subtle. Like erosion.

But here's what I've learned:

I don't need their recognition to be real.

I don't need their invitation to belong to myself.

Ceres teaches care—but she also teaches **release**.

And Saturn teaches structure—but also **boundaries**.

So as I write this, I'm allowing myself to say what I once wouldn't: *I don't care if I never see them again.*

Not because I'm cold. But because **I'm done freezing myself to make others feel warm.**

I am choosing different soil.

And that choice is not bitterness.

It is liberation.

The Fall and the Pope

As this conjunction built, I pulled a card from the Red Threads Tarot: **The Fall**. How fitting.

Not the Fall as failure. The Fall as surrender. The Fall as necessary descent.

Part 10: The Last Harvest: Ceres, Saturn—Beginnings and Endings

At the same time, a new Pope was elected. In the shadow of crumbling systems and centuries of trauma, the cardinals chose a new face of spiritual care. I am not one to place faith in patriarchal institutions. But even I felt a ripple. An opening.

What does it mean that this decision came as **Ceres and Saturn approached 29° Pisces?** The end of the zodiac. The culmination of karma.

In myth, Ceres lost her daughter to the underworld. But she did not collapse. She demanded justice. She changed the seasons. She rewrote the terms.

Now, in this cycle, she is walking with Saturn not as a subordinate . . . but as a sovereign.

This moment is not about institutional redemption. It is about archetypal rearrangement. Ceres is at the table now, even if the men in robes don't know her name. She is moving through the roots of the system. Quietly. Unstoppably.

Closing Threads

Ceres and Saturn at 29° Pisces ask us:

- What grief have you not yet named?
- What cycle are you being asked to end, even if no one else understands?
- What truth are you ready to lay down, not in defeat, but in devotion?

This is not collapse. This is compost. This is not abandonment. This is release.

There are endings we don't choose, and endings we walk toward with sacred clarity. This, I believe, is the latter.

We are not here to feed systems that starve us. We are here to choose new soil, new stories, and new sources of care.

This is the last harvest.

And beyond it? Beginnings await.

Reflection Prompt: Where in your own life are you being invited to let go, even if it's hard? What harvest is complete? What grief is asking to be named before something new can begin?

What Might This Mean?

This long arc—from the first conjunction at 0° Aries to the second at 0° Aquarius—bookends a collective initiation. It suggests a transformation from self-centered independence (Aries) to visionary interdependence (Aquarius). The feminine, in her many forms, is rising not just in visibility but in leadership.

Ceres, alongside Venus and Pluto, reminds us:

- We must grieve what has been lost and destroyed.
- We must reclaim the power of nurturance and emotional wisdom.
- We must value the Earth not as resource, but as kin.

This conjunction may also be a turning point for the United States— echoing its founding themes, calling it to embody a more integrated

Part 10: The Last Harvest: Ceres, Saturn—Beginnings and Endings

vision of power, care, and freedom.

We are living in the era that Ceres, Venus, and Pluto began seeding over two centuries ago. Now, their convergence at the cusp of Aquarius offers a call to weave a new story—one that honors the cycles of life, the wisdom of the feminine, and the promise of collective rebirth

---

Sidebar: The Asteroid Goddesses as Archetypal Allies

In the early 1800s, four powerful feminine bodies were discovered in close succession: Ceres (1801), Pallas Athena (1802), Juno (1804), and Vesta (1807). Known as the asteroid goddesses, they represent distinct yet complementary aspects of the feminine:

- Ceres: The Great Mother, nourisher, and guardian of the cycles of life, grief, and renewal.
- Pallas Athena: The strategist, wisdom keeper, and protector of just causes.
- Juno: The sacred partner, reflecting commitment, fairness, and sovereignty within relationships.
- Vesta: The hearth keeper, guardian of the inner flame, and channel for spiritual devotion.

Together, they form a sacred quartet—offering insight into how feminine energy shows up in various dimensions of life. While this book focuses on Ceres, her relationship with these other celestial sisters is part of a larger reawakening of the feminine in astrology.

Astrologers may wish to track how all four work together in a chart, weaving a tapestry of inner wisdom, outer power, and sacred service. Their rise coincides with a time when humanity is being asked to honor care, cooperation, creativity, and community as essential evolutionary forces.

Part 11: Case Studies—Ceres in Living Charts

Witnessing her in others helps us recognize her in ourselves.

Exploring real-life examples can help us see how Ceres functions in the lived stories of public figures. The following case studies offer insight into how her themes of nurturing, loss, empowerment, and service can play out on the world stage.

Greta Thunberg – Ceres in Aries (no accurate birth time)

Environmental activist Greta Thunberg expresses Ceres in Aries through fierce advocacy, bold action, and courageous truth-telling. Aries nurtures through fire—by protecting what matters, charging into conflict when necessary, and refusing to be silenced in the face of injustice. Greta's activism embodies the warrior side of Ceres: unyielding, urgent, and driven by instinct.

Ceres in Aries often cares by confronting harm head-on. Greta's refusal to placate authority figures and her willingness to speak uncomfortable truths reflect this placement's raw, protective energy. Her fight for the Earth mirrors Ceres' mythic rage—the kind that stops time itself until what's sacred is restored.

Princess Diana – Ceres in Taurus (4th House)

Princess Diana, often referred to as the "People's Princess," had Ceres in Taurus in the 4th house. Taurus reflects grounding, physical care, and comfort, while the 4th house is the domain of home, roots, and ancestral patterns. Diana's nurturing was deeply physical and embodied—she was known for hugging AIDS patients, advocating for landmine victims, and being an emotionally present mother to her children.

Her Ceres placement reflects a need to offer safety and physical touch in her role as mother—not only to her sons, but to the world. Taurus also speaks to Diana's love of beauty, gardens, and the simple pleasures that grounded her through public upheaval. Her tragic loss echoed the grief of Ceres herself—and her legacy continues to inspire conversations about emotional openness, maternal presence, and compassion in public life.

Michelle Obama - Ceres in Sagittarius (no accurate birth time)

Michelle Obama's Ceres in Sagittarius reveals a nurturing style grounded in wisdom, vision, and expansive care. Sagittarius speaks to truth-telling, empowerment, and the freedom to grow. Ceres in this sign seeks to nourish through possibility—uplifting others by widening their horizons and encouraging self-discovery.

As First Lady, Michelle championed wellness, education, and liberation through knowledge. Her initiatives like the White House Kitchen Garden and the "Let's Move" campaign reflect Sagittarian values: proactive health, lifelong learning, and joyful embodiment. Her memoir *Becoming* offered further nourishment—modeling self-reflection, resilience, and personal evolution.

Ceres in Sagittarius nurtures by opening doors, not enclosing them. Michelle's legacy is one of inspiring others to thrive through purpose, truth, and the courage to expand beyond limitation.

Pope Leo - Ceres in Capricorn (House Unknown)

Pope Leo was born with Ceres in Capricorn, conjunct Chariklo and trine his Mars in Virgo. While we don't have a birth time to determine house placement, Ceres in Capricorn speaks to caregiving through structure, responsibility, and sustained effort. This is a placement of protective authority—nurturing through leadership, order, and long-term commitment. The conjunction with Chariklo, the sacred witness and space-holder, suggests an ability to hold grief and healing in silent strength. His trine to Mars in Virgo indicates a service-oriented path where action is aligned with devotion and humility. Elected under the Saturn–North Node–Ceres conjunction in Pisces, Pope Leo may represent a quiet restoration of sacred care in global systems. His chart hints at a papacy grounded in stewardship, ritual, and the return of respect for the rhythms of the Earth and spirit.

Prince Harry - Ceres in Taurus (4th House)

Prince Harry has Ceres in Taurus in the 4th house, conjunct his Moon and North Node. Ceres in Taurus nurtures through stability, presence, and a deep reverence for the natural world and the body. In the 4th house, these themes turn inward—toward home, ancestry, and emotional security. The conjunction to the Moon and North Node intensifies the pull toward emotional healing and the reclamation of a more grounded, heart-centered way of being.

Harry's journey reflects this Ceres signature vividly. The loss of his mother shaped a lifelong quest to create a different kind of family legacy—one rooted in safety, honesty, and love. His decisions to step back from royal life and publicly address mental health issues align with this placement's need to nourish from the roots upward. Ceres here calls for a return to embodied care and emotional truth—especially within the masculine lineage.

These case studies illuminate how Ceres speaks through not only personal nurturing styles, but through cultural roles, losses, and acts of service. Whether through speech or touch, activism or devotion, Ceres moves through us in deeply personal and often profoundly public ways.

Appendix A: Expanded Exercises for Working with Ceres

Releasing to Receive

- Light a white or green candle and sit quietly under the full moon. Reflect on what you've been carrying that no longer feeds you. Write these down, then offer them to the Earth—bury them, burn them, or place them under a stone with intention.
- Invite Ceres to guide you through this release. What nourishment wants to grow in the new space you've created?

Shamanic Journey Prompt

- Set sacred space. Use a drum, rattle, or playlist to guide you.
- Ask to meet the part of yourself that knows how to tend life. This may appear as a wise elder, a gardener, a midwife, a wild animal, or even the Earth herself.
- Ask: What am I here to nourish? What does my spirit most need now?
- Record your insights afterward through writing, art, or dance.

Daily Integration Practice

- Keep a "nourishment journal" for one week. At the end of each day, reflect: What truly nourished me today? What depleted me? What small act of care could I offer myself tomorrow?

Appendix B: Ceres Keywords & Associations

Themes

- Nourishment, nurturing, caregiving, protection
- Grief, loss, reunion, cycles of life and death
- Renewal, sustainability, sacred transitions
- Embodiment, fertility, motherhood, parenthood
- Emotional labor, devotion, body wisdom

Domains of Influence

- Food, farming, herbs, cooking, gardening
- Family systems, early bonding, emotional resilience
- Natural rhythms, menstruation, menopause, seasonal rites
- Land stewardship, environmental care, holistic living

Gifts of Ceres

- Deep empathy and care for others
- Strong instincts for healing and tending
- Ability to transform loss into wisdom
- Power to ground and stabilize through change

Challenges of Ceres

- Over-identifying with caretaker roles
- Emotional enmeshment or martyrdom
- Difficulty receiving care or setting boundaries
- Feeling abandoned, unseen, or unworthy of nurture

Symbols & Archetypes

- The Great Mother
- The Gardener
- The Midwife
- The Earth Keeper
- The Grieving Mother

This appendix offers a condensed reference point for Ceres' rich symbolic language. Use it as a guidepost as you continue to explore her presence in your chart and your life.

Conclusion: A Return to Sacred Care

Ceres is not just an asteroid, a dwarf planet, or a forgotten goddess re-entering our skies—she is a cosmic presence calling us home. Her return to prominence in astrology echoes something deeper: the rebirth of cyclical wisdom, ancestral memory, and earth-based care. Through every chart and transit, Ceres reminds us that healing is not linear, and nourishment is not optional. It is sacred. It is essential.

To include Ceres in our astrology is to reclaim astrology itself as a healing art—one that feeds the soul and guides us back into relationship with life, death, and the mysteries in between.

May this book be an offering toward that return.

Author's Note

This book was not simply written—it was remembered. It came through long walks under stars, whispered dreams, and ancestral echoes. I wrote it not only as an astrologer, but as a daughter, a mother, and a weaver of myth and meaning. My hope is that it nourishes you, awakens something old and tender within you, and helps you walk more gently and courageously in the world.

With love and gratitude, Louise (Lumina, The Cosmic Owl)

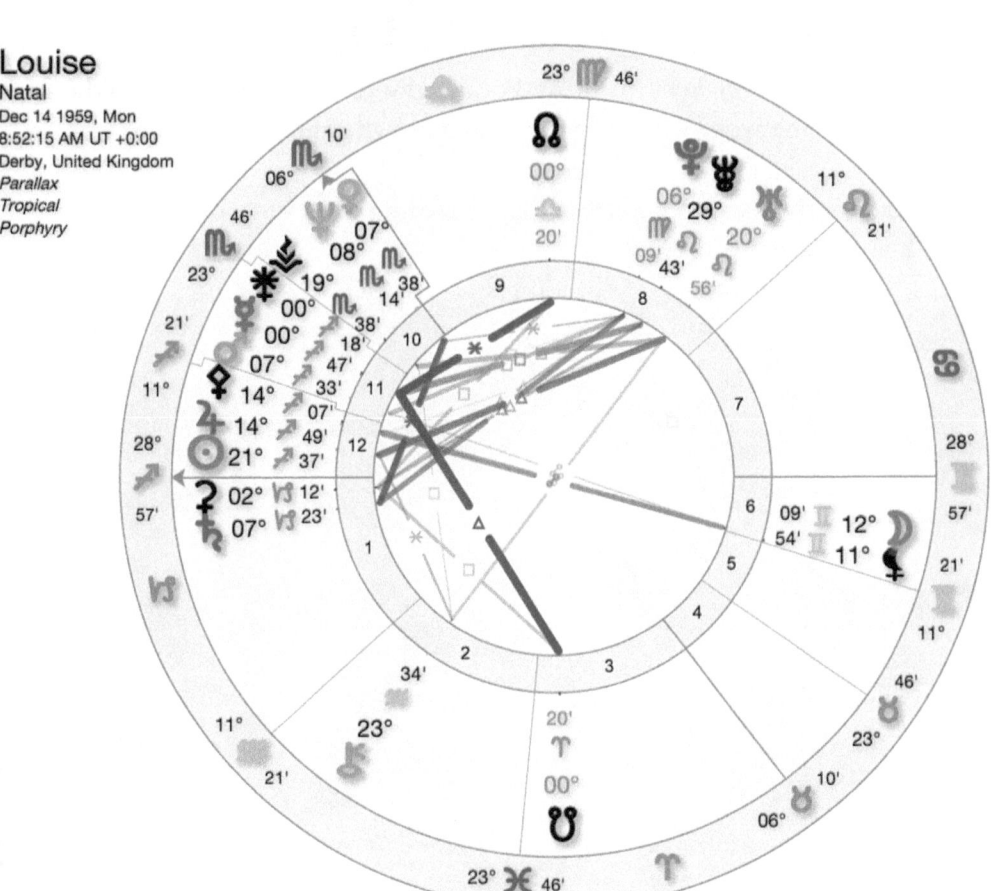

Dedication

For the ones who kept the seeds. For the grandmothers who sang to the wheat. For anyone who has grieved, and grown, and grieved again.

And for the Earth, who never stopped feeding us—even when we forgot how to listen.

Sacred Resources & References
Sacred Sources

These texts, voices, and echoes have nourished this work.

- The Homeric Hymn to Demeter – Translated in many forms, including the Loeb Classical Library edition.
- Sappho, Fragment 147 – Translations by Anne Carson and Mary Barnard.
- Hymn to Inanna by Enheduanna – From *Inanna: Lady of Largest Heart*, trans. Betty De Shong Meador.
- Friedrich Schiller's "Hymn to Joy" – Cited in *The Brothers Karamazov* by Fyodor Dostoyevsky.
- Asteroid Goddesses by Demetra George and Douglas Bloch.
- "Ceres: The Dark Harvest" by Dawn Bodrogi – from *The Inner Wheel* (archived website).
- NASA's Dawn Mission – https://science.nasa.gov/mission/dawn/
- Bethany Webster on The Mother Wound – https://www.bethanywebster.com
- Pandora Astrology's Ceres rulership case – https://pandoraastrology.com/ceres-rules-taurus/

About the Author

Louise Edington, known as *The Cosmic Owl* or *Lumina*, is a visionary astrologer, author, and sacred storyteller who has spent over three decades studying the stars and the soul. Her work weaves deep myth, evolutionary astrology, and quantum consciousness into transformative pathways of healing and empowerment.

She is the author of *The Complete Guide to Astrology, Modern Astrology, The Complete Guide to Tarot and Astrology*, and *Ceres in Astrology: Nourishment, Power, and the Rebirth of the Feminine*. As a passionate teacher, she leads courses and retreats that awaken soul remembrance and cosmic connection.

Through her online offerings, mentorship circles, and daily writing, Lumina helps seekers reconnect with the wisdom of the Earth, the rhythms of the cosmos, and the regenerative power of the divine feminine.

She is the founder of *The Cosmic Owl*, a daily astrology and tarot transmission, and *The Nest*, a private community for astrological deepening and collective transformation. Her work is devoted to reweaving astrology as a tool of empowerment, reclamation, and sacred care.

Her unique voice bridges ancient archetypes with the future of astrology—one sacred thread at a time.

Ceres Timeline of Archetypal Evolution

This timeline offers a brief sweep through the mythic, astronomical, and collective milestones that mark Ceres' journey—from forgotten goddess to cosmic guide.

- 9000–6000 BCE – The Great Mother appears in early agrarian cultures across Old Europe and the Near East, long before her myth is codified as Demeter.
- 3000 BCE – Her story begins taking written shape in proto-Indo-European and early Greek traditions. Mythic origin: Demeter and Persephone's story emerges.
- 496 BCE - Cult of Ceres introduced to Rome, along with the cults of Liber and Libera (the Roman counterparts of Dionysus and Persephone).
- 493 BCE - A temple dedicated to Ceres, Liber, and Libera was built on the Aventine Hill in 493 BC, becoming a center of plebeian religious and political activity.
- 1801 – Dwarf Planet Ceres is discovered and briefly named a planet.
- 1823 – Ceres–Venus–Pluto conjunction at 0° Aries (World Axis): a gateway moment.
- 1850s – Removed from the planetary list as smaller asteroids are discovered.

- 2006 – Reclassified as a dwarf planet the same day Pluto was demoted.
- 2024 – Ceres–Venus–Pluto conjunction at 0° Aquarius, initiating a collective reawakening.
- 2025 – This book is born under a powerful Ceres–North Node–Saturn conjunction in Pisces: Ceres in Astrology: Nourishment, Power, and the Rebirth of the Feminine. A cosmic invitation to restore sacred care, ancestral memory, and collective responsibility.

Let this thread of remembrance guide you as you explore the sacred return of care, grief, nourishment, and transformation.

www.ingramcontent.com/pod-product-compliance
Lightning Source LLC
Chambersburg PA
CBHW020248010526
44107CB00002B/162